All Being Well

PATIENCE STRONG

All Being Well

All being well we will meet for tea. Next
Friday as usual, the arrangement will be –
same place and same table – at quarter past
three . . . All being well.

Three little words, but how much they can
mean – Acknowledging humbly that
things unforeseen – can crash in on life,
changing plans, wrecking schemes –
perhaps for our good though untimely it
seems . . . Three little words. They're a
prayer in a shell: God willing – If possible –
All being well.

Just in Time

Just in time is time enough for setting matters straight – because if you are just in time you cannot be too late – for patching up a quarrel when bad feelings have been stirred – burying the hatchet with a letter or a word.

Tomorrow is a day too late to mend a broken heart, or to save a friendship when the bonds have come apart . . . Today the severed links you can repair and reunite. Today you may be just in time to put the wrong thing right.

The Loveliest Time of the Day

The loveliest time of the day – is the time
when its glory grows dim – and long
feathered clouds glowing golden and
crimson hang over the earth's distant rim
... The heart gathers peace with the
deepening dusk and the mind sheds its
cares one by one – troubles seem less, all
the unhappy things slip away, going down
with the sun.

O may the evening of life's little day bring
the blessing of inward content – as you
start to discover a new way of living, false
pleasures and passions all spent ... You
find that delusions no longer delight and
your dreams you can dream without tears
– other horizons will loom into sight as
you live out the best of the years.

There is a Way for You

There is a way. Keep looking and you'll
find it. A mountain blocks your vision, but
behind it – a valley opens out into a view –
that seems to have been waiting there for
you. There is a pass – between the hills you
trace it. There is a path. It's rough, but if
you face it – believing in the thing for
which you pray – you'll reach the peak you
seek. There is a way.

Someone Trusts You

Someone trusts you. Someone puts great
confidence in you – knowing that the thing
you say is wise and right and true . . .
Someone needs you when it seems that
everything is wrong – needs your arm to
lean upon when roads are hard and long.
Someone loves you. Somebody pays heed
to what you say. Think before you speak
the hurried word and turn away.
Somebody is counting on your love and
sympathy. Make the time to listen, and to
listen patiently.

There is a Way

There is a way of saying things that does not leave behind – memories that linger in the corners of the mind – bringing at some future time an echo of regret – that follows you along the years: the words you can't forget.

There is a way to speak: the way of peace and harmony – that leaves no hurt within the heart: Love's way of charity . . . There is a way of living that if practised faithfully – could change the world: the Master plan of Christianity.

The Spur of the Moment

When the spur of the moment sends an impulse to the brain – we can spring forward in swift response or passively remain – to give the thing a second thought, reflecting quietly. Which is the wiser course – to leap ahead or wait and see? Examine the moments that prompt your thoughts before you start to act. Moments that quicken anger call for humour and for tact. Moments of sudden awareness of another's agony – goad us to test the limits of our generosity . . . Hour by hour within us good and evil passions stir – but safely can you act at the moment when Love applies the spur.

Bless the Day

Bless the day when it comes to your window – stealing in on the edge of the night ... Whether it's grey and shrouded in shadow – or sapphire and gold in the first morning light.

Bless the day with a heart that is singing – as with hope the fresh prospect is viewed ... Bless the day for the good it is bringing – Run to greet it with courage renewed.

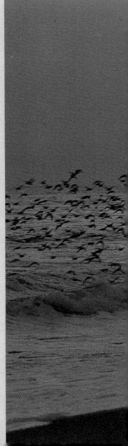

Scattered Clouds

The clouds are torn and tattered as the
wind goes screaming by – ragged strips are
scattered, blown like rooks about the sky –
by angry gusts that shake the house and
shudder through the room – But out there,
if you look, you'll see a gold crack in the
gloom – a glimpse of glory from the source
of everlasting light – reminds you that
behind the doom-black darkness – all is
bright.

It may be that your small world is rocked
by storms today. Troubles are like moving
clouds – They come, but not to stay . . .
tomorrow – or the next day there'll be
happier things in view – the golden cracks
will open out to let the sun come through.

One Ray of Sunshine

One ray of sunshine can change a whole
day – One flash of gold stealing out of the
grey – Can warm a cold heart as a fire
warms the hands – Hope is set free and
releases its bands – and Love like a root
buried deep out of sight – stirs in its sleep
and awakes to the light.

Is it not strange that the sun as it falls – on
prisons and gardens and windows and
walls – can so lift the spirit from out of the
mire – and set it aglow with delight and
desire.

To Greet Another Spring

The autumn trees are weeping for they
know the bitter truth – that they must say
goodbye to summer and the year's green
youth . . . Leaves of amber, flame and gold
are scattered carelessly – by the winds that
bring the season of austerity.

Unlike the trees, I cannot grieve when
bright leaves fall and fade – because I know
that nature's laws must ever be obeyed – so
that in the hardened veins of every living
thing – the April sap can rise again to greet
another Spring.

One Day's Journey

Go your way with one day's load – but not along tomorrow's road. You are not asked to walk that track – until it's on the almanac. Until today has faded out – you do not need to think about – what tomorrow's going to bring. A good thought, that, to which to cling.

Do not face until you must – tomorrow's problems – Let the dust – of one day's troubles settle first. Don't anticipate the worst. When the going's rough and tough – One day's journey is enough.

After a
Good Night's Sleep

Don't take your troubles to bed with you –
they'll never let you sleep. Leave them all
outside the door. Exclude them. They will
keep – and be ready to spring at you when
darkness slips away – as you open the door
once more upon another day.

But if you've slept well and if you've had a
deep and perfect rest – you will be able to
deal with them, for you will know how
best – to think and speak and act when
worries nag at you ding-dong – mastering
every problem as and when it comes along.

Paved with Gold

In this our temperate island home the
pathway of the year – is paved with
Nature's golden gifts that month by
month appear: January's aconites,
bright-eyed, frilled glossy green –
February's carpeting of woodland
celandine. March's crocus candles. April's
daffodils in bloom. May's laburnum.
Golden June, gorse, buttercups and
broom.
July: gaillardias, lilies, dahlias and
nasturtiums. August wheat, September
sunflowers. So the Autumn comes –
October birch, November beech their
cloaks of splendour fling – around
December as it runs to greet the Christmas
King.

Just a Little

A little help goes a long long way when it's just the help you need. A little word quite a lot can say – one little word can feed – your hungry heart with a single crumb when you sit alone with your tears – wondering what became of all the lost and lonely years.

One little morsel of broken bread an aching void can fill – and send you out with your strength renewed to climb the next great hill . . . One little measure of kindliness can calm and comfort you – and bring you out of the pit to find the world made fresh and new.

Always the Best

Always look your best though no-one else is there to see. Always make the best of things wherever you may be. Always put your best into the job you have to do – Place the best construction on what's said or done to you.

Always play your best though no-one's there to keep the score. Always show your best face when there's someone at the door. The best foot forward gets you home – you do not need to run. Always see the best and not the worst in everyone.